NEW PATIENT SCHOOL

SAM CARLSON

NEW PATIENT SCHOOL

The How To Guide For Converting More Leads Into Patients

Patient Stream LLC

Patient Stream LLC

CONTENTS

1. Getting Started
2. The Practice Simulator & Lead Tracker
3. Lead Volume Protocol
4. Patient Stream Follow Up Protocol
5. The Daily Marketer Script
6. Appointment Confirmation Protocol
7. Call Confirmation Protocol
8. Day 1 Protocols
9. Day 2 Protocol
10. Five Step Report of Findings

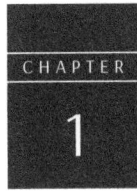

GETTING STARTED

Hello! My name is Sam Carlson and I am the creator of this guide. I have created it as a roadmap to help you master converting leads into patients. Over the course of 4 years as a Practice Consultant as well as a Digital Marketing Consultant, I collected and created different aspects of this guide. It was, and will continue to be a work in progress as more new tactics are able to be added with the end goal of helping you, the user.

While I wrote much of this, I learned the most valuable parts from friends and mentors with proven track records and giving hearts. I would like to acknowledge their critical roles in the creation of this work.

Dr. Sunny Gill

Dr. Gill was my first mentor in the Chiropractic space. He is a successful practice owner and taught me how to run a clinic at the start of my time working with practices across the country.

Many of the systems, protocols and scripts originate from him in one way or another. He is an amazing man, great friend, and ridiculously talented business person.

Dr. Andrew Wells

Dr. Wells and I met back in 2019 when he attended Dr. Chad Woolner's M.A.P Event in Boise, Idaho. He is incredibly smart and, like Dr. Gill, willing to share his experience and systems with our users as well.

Our New Patient School trainings would not have been possible were it not for his willingness to share his knowledge and systems he used to build several 7-figure practices.

To You!

This guide is meant to be a living document. You will notice there are several places throughout its pages where you can make notes and adaptations to fit your practice. Please feel free to share your insights with us so we can help others successfully build what we are all striving to create.

The Future You Deserve!

Now, let's get started.

WELCOME TO PATIENT STREAM

When it comes to growing your business with leads, you're going to need a set of "blueprints" to work from. A way to solve any problem you may encounter, not to mention a proven methods to train and prepare as you grow and expand.

Enter the New Patient School Guide to Converting Leads Into Patients.

This document was designed to serve as your practice's foundation to building a business that attracts and enrolls new patients every month. In it you will find proven systems either used during my consulting career or those that were learned from other professionals with proven track records.

So, if you are new to systems, let's make sure we understand that first.

Systems: a good system has a written overview (protocol), a target outcome (stat desired) a tactical approach (script, how to), and implementation (training & exercises)

Within this guide you will encounter multiple systems. It is your job to train, use, and optimize them so you can get the desired outcome you are striving for.

RESOURCES

This guide references several guides, forms, and trainings. For a full list of resources and to access, go to: **www.mypatientstream.com/book**

UNDERSTANDING LEADS

Some people have mixed feelings about leads when they don't understand how to use them. On the other hand, businesses that understand what a lead is and how to use them, can literally unlock the growth potential at will.

So, what is a lead?

When you run marketing campaigns using Patient Stream what you are going after are "Qualified Leads".

A Qualified Lead constitutes any individual who raises their hand signaling they identify with a specific condition. Our Ads and Offers are designed to:

- Attract "Qualified Attention"
- AND Advance the Sale (not make the sale)

When it comes to increasing their desire and motivation... There is no replacement for personal interaction.

People buy from people.

UNDERSTANDING OFFERS

If you are looking to get new patients in quantity, making the right offers can unlock potential growth when you need it.

If you are nervous to discount a service because you're not making enough on that visit, it may help to understand these two principles:

Front end money: Front end money is the fee you conceded within the initial part of the sales process. These fees are not meant to make you a bunch of money, in fact, some will even cause you to lose money. This money is a small concession you make in exchange for your prospects' time and interest.

Back end money: Back end money is the money you earn after a prospect converts into a fully paid patient. To maximize back end money, you need to show prospects how you can solve their problem(s), educate to the point of belief, and provide a clear path to close.

Here is the point...

A good offer is your best friend.

It can supply a lot of leads which can lead to a great deal of patients.

STATS... YOUR BEST FRIEND

Tracking your stats is the most efficient business growth tool you will ever have.

Why?

Every stat represents a system that is either not working, needs to be adapted, or is not being followed.

In this guide we will teach you:

- What your target STATS should be
- The systems that control your STATS
- How to fix problems if things go wrong

When you know your stats, can identify your problems, and solve them quickly...

You will have what every business longs for...

CONTROL!

THE END GOAL

When you sign up as a Patient Stream user, we have a singular goal:

Help you get more Patients!

By utilizing our growing library of Click-Campaigns, Guides, trainings (like this one), and amazing support staff, you will experience first-hand the effort and care we have put in to helping you achieve your goals.

So, if you ever feel confused or stuck...

We're here for you.

Once again, welcome to Patient Stream.

Sam Carlson
And the Patient Stream Team

PRACTICE SIMULATOR
QUESTIONNAIRE:

_____

Before you begin using the Practice Simulator, it is helpful to gather the data needed to finish this exercise. Please follow the instruction below so you can complete the Simulator quickly.

Instructions: Answer the 5 questions below for ease of use as you utilize the Practice Simulator and Lead Tracker.

1. Over the previous 30 day period, how many new patients did your practice add?_____
2. What were your total month collections for this time-frame?_____
3. How many total patient visits did you see (new and existing)?_____
4. How many leads did you have in this time-frame? (If nothing, answer 50)_____
5. How much did you spend on Advertising for those leads? (If nothing answer 1200)_____

Now that you have answered these questions, simply go to the simulator and enter the values in the appropriate spots. The only other values you will need to enter are your targets in Step 3. This step is easily completed on the simulator once you have entered the values above.

THE PRACTICE SIMULATOR & LEAD TRACKER

Using the Practice Simulator & Lead Tracker is the key to fixing bottlenecks in your practice.

Here is how to begin.

- There are cells that need manual inputs (marked in blue)
- And cells that provide outputs (marked in green)

Now, let's walk through the Simulator in the correct order to show you how it works.

Step 1: Establishing Your Practice Baseline

Start this process by getting an idea of where your business is right now.

Step 1: Base-line	30 Day Time-Frame	
	New Patients	38
	Collections	$61,234.00
	Total # Visits	715
	New Patient Stat	38
	Patient Visit Avg.	18.82
	Per Visit Value	$85.64
	Per Case Value	$1,611.42

Note: This tool uses a 30 day time frame, which for some practices can be an issue. For the most part, however, we still find that these numbers provide valuable information. You can certainly use the tool to evaluate a longer time-frame if you choose.

Here are the inputs needed:

The number of new patients for the 30 day period being evaluated.

The amount collected for both cash and insurance.

The total visits for that time frame.

What the outputs mean:

Patient Visit Average (PVA): This is the average number of visits per patient.

Per Visit Value: This is the avg. value of a visit in your clinic.

Per Case Value: This is what a new patient is worth in your Practice.

Note: Most industries have established baselines for the figures above. Knowing where your practice should be in relationship to the industry is important for growing your practice. Find a trusted coach, colleague to make sure you know what those numbers are.

Step 2: STATS

Enter your current data with regard to lead performance. If you are not currently getting leads, you can enter lead values based on our current performance.

IE: 50 Leads/Mo - $1100 Spend.

	Lead Volume	Appts Set	Show Rate	Day 1 to 2	Enroll %
STAT	100%	70% Great / 60% Goal	70%	80%	80%
WEEK 1	12	4	3	3	2
	12	33.33	75.00	100.00	66.67

To complete this section, you will need to enter each weeks performance over 30 past days as follows:

· Lead Volume: How many leads did you get in this time period?

· Appointments Set: How many appointments were set from those leads?
· Show Rate: Of the appointments set, how many showed up?
· Day 1 - Day 2: How many advanced from their first appointment to the second?
· Enrollment Rate: How many turned into Patients?

The Target Stat for each is listed above the cell.

Off to the right you will also see a blue cell under Ad spend. Grab your credit card statement or however you keep track and put in the amount.

Ad Spend
$1,188.00
$79.20

Once you have done this, you will have your cost to acquire a new patient (in green) , and be ready to move to the next step.

Step 3: Creating Your Target

We now have everything we need to map out our growth plan. In this step we will set a target and reverse engineer our path to success.

Step 3: Target	Practice Simulator	
	Additional New Patients	14
	Projected Total Revenue	$83,793.89
	Projected Total Visits	978

We all have different goals, but in this example, we wanted to shoot for the much coveted 7-Figure practice.

So, at $83,793.89/mo we will hit that mark.

The big question is how?

The answer comes next.

Step 4: The Simulator

Here is where things should really start to get exciting. Once we know our goal, we know what STATS to manage to reach it, and we can confidently start taking action to achieve the outcome.

Our key take-aways from this final step are our Daily Budget and Total Leads Needed to hit our mark.

Daily/Mo Budget: This amount is what we project to spend every day/month on lead generation as we move towards our goal.

Lead Volume: Ultimately our growth relies on this STAT. We cannot hit our new patient numbers without managing this leading metric. So, we want to track this number weekly and make modifications to our approach if we are not hitting our target numbers.

KNOWING YOUR NUMBERS

Tracking our numbers is empowering but it can also make some anxious. Let's get a healthy perspective on how to use them.

First and foremost, we are most concerned about the compounding effects of our efforts over time. Expecting to change our practice in 30-90 days, while possible, is not a realistic expectation.

It is kind of like expecting to lose weight, obtain optimal health, and never have to worry about dieting again after just 30-90 days.

Here is what reality looks like:

· You will have some weeks where leads are down, stats are in the toilet, and you are left scratching your head.

· You will have some offers that perform like magic and others that do not work nearly as well.

· You will have leads who are not interested immediately and others who act like they never opted-in in the first place!

You will also have:

· Low-cost / high volume campaigns, great STATS, and convert to care with ease.

· Smooth growth weeks where everything seems to go right.

· People who love you and are so grateful for what you are doing to help them.

All of these scenarios are likely to happen and it is important to remember the following:

· Consistency ALWAYS compounds.

· Building an audience of both Prospects and Patients is what real marketing is about.

· The Practice you have now WILL NOT become the Practice you want without change.

· And when the naysayers get in your ear, remember this simple response...

"Shhh, I'm Building Something."

MARKET ANALYZER

Instructions: List the conditions you'd like to promote in your practice. Then preview the list of Click-Campaigns available and list then in the box provided. Once you prove a campaign, list it in the control box. And if the offer does not perform, place it in the stand-by box.

Note: All Click-Campaigns have been proven to work, but they will perform differently from market to market. Your best course of action is to focus on offers that include some type of treatment. While there are times where we may have campaigns that do not include treatment, they are primarily for testing.

CONDITIONS

CONTROLS

CLICK-CAMPAIGNS

STAND-BY

BEFORE MOVING ON TO LEAD PROTOCOLS

How to achieve optimal lead volume so you can hit your Practice's new patient goal.

Mindset: The Lead Volume Protocol is designed to help you learn how lead generation will work in your location as well as help you build a plan so you can predictably add new patients every month.

Since no two practices are the same, and because no 2 offers will produce equal results, finding your niche(s) will be of great value to your overall success.

Please begin this protocol by writing in your desired Lead Volume STAT on the line above.

Lead Volume Protocol_____
Lead Stacking Protocol_____
Market Analyzer Sheet_____

LEAD VOLUME PROTOCOL

Objective:

To build a monthly system capable of hitting your target lead volume and grow a finding pool month after month. Our goal is to find 3 campaigns available for use when needed. This will allow us to turn off underperforming campaigns and still have 2 others ready to step in if needed.

Point of Interest:

While Patient Stream does have offers which do NOT include a treatment, the campaigns that perform the best most often offer something to patients. When positioned properly, offering treatments is actually to your advantage because education is best received through demonstration. Offers that do not include treatment may work in some areas but should be tested for effectiveness in your market. Do NOT run an offer without a treatment until you have proven a minimum of 3 other offers.

Tactical Approach:

List your top conditions desired for new patient growth and list them on the following **"Market Analyzer"** document.

- Launch 1-2 Click-Campaigns with a minimum budget of $40/Day per campaign.
- Wait 1 week and evaluate your results.

If you are happy with the production, write the offer(s) into the **"Control"** section of the Market Analyzer.

If you are not happy, move it to the **"Stand-by"** section for later testing and start the next Click-Campaign on your Market Analyzer.

In the event that you are not satisfied with either one of your two initial campaigns, reach out to support for additional help and troubleshooting.

Goal:

By the end of month two you should have 3 or more Control Campaigns you can use to get leads for our services. Use these Control Campaigns and continue the testing process as needed.

LEAD STACKING PROTOCOL

Overview:

The primary goal of Lead Stacking is to maintain a steady flow of leads as well as be able to kick lead volume into high gear if desired. Lead Stacking is a strategy that involves layering "Control" campaigns for the purposes of lead consistency and increase volume.

Tactical Approach:

Step 1: Launch a Click-Campaign from your control list. If you do not have a Control list yet, you will want to complete the "Market Analyzer" first.

Step 2: Wait approximately 2 weeks and layer in a second campaign.

Step 3: Monitor lead cost and production. Once a campaign begins to decline, you can either choose to turn that campaign off and re-launch a similar (same niche) campaign OR you can layer in another one of your Control campaigns.

Note: poor campaign production can be a product of an audience being tired of an offer and ready for a new one, because the algorithm has lost steam, or it might just be time to switch things up. No need to be concerned just turn the campaign off and start your next one.

Note: It is best practices not to exceed 2 active lead generation campaigns at any given point in time. Flooding the marketing with too many offers has not historically provided additional benefit, rather caused overall performance to suffer.

Back Pain   Knee Pain

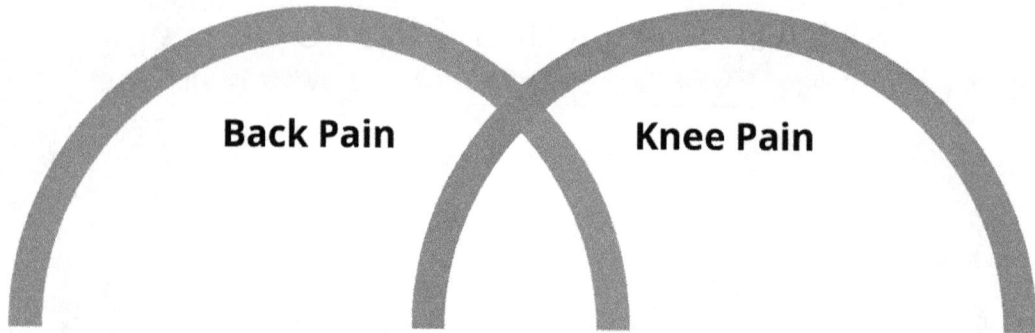

STACKING LEAD CAMPAIGNS

LEAD TO APPOINTMENT STAT

70% Amazing - 60% Target

How to follow-up with leads using automation, scripting, and daily lead management efforts.

Mindset: The Lead to Appointment Protocol is designed to help you maximize your follow-up process. Our goal here is to focus both on the short-term follow-up system as well as long-term re-engagement of past leads and patients.

The STATS above are what we shoot for, but can be challenging to attain during the first 30-60 days. As your lead pool increases, and you improve your execution of these protocols, so will your appointment set rate.

Use the checklist below to ensure quality control as you implement.

Checklist:

- · Patient Stream Personalizations_____
- · Potential Optimizations_____
- · Lead Calling Protocol_____
- · The Daily Marketer Script_____

PATIENT STREAM FOLLOW UP PROTOCOL

Objective:

To customize and personalize our follow-up automation provided in Patient Stream. While the pre-built campaigns are functional, personalizing each has proven to be very effective in increasing response.

Tactical Approach:

- All Click-Campaigns in Patient Stream have pre-built follow up automations (email/texting) designed to communicate with leads as soon as they opt-in. So, begin this protocol by verifying you have requested and activated the follow-up automation specific to your Ad campaign. (Instructions can be found in the Patient Stream Users Guide located at www.mypatientstream.com/book)

- To maximize your follow-up efforts and increase the level of response, we recommend you Edit and personalize the pre-built messages in the follow-up campaign
- Monitor all lead responses and respond within 5 minutes when Follow the Lead Calling Protocol to reach a 60% Appt rate.
- In many cases, responding to leads during business hours will be adequate. However, if at any time your Lead to Appt stat falls, you many consider extending your hours by using the Patient Stream App to respond.

Goal:

Increase lead response numbers using a more personalized approach and ultimately hitting our response rate so we can get an Appointment Set rate at or above 60%.

Note: If you are not hitting the STATS needed see the following Potential Optimizations.

POTENTIAL FOLLOW UP
OPTIMIZATIONS

Changing the initial follow-up message is a good way to improve response rate. For a full tutorial and explanation please watch the follow-up tutorial video on the resource page.

Meet them- Approach #1 Engage

The goal of engaging a lead is to solicit a response. That is what we are going for.

Ask a question: Text 1 "Hi Sam, this is Jacob from PS Clinic..."

5 seconds later Text 2 "Sorry to hear about your Knee pain. What part of the Knee is hurting most?"

Or maybe: "Text 1 "Hi Sam, my name is Jacob with PS Clinic..."

5 seconds later Text 2 "Is it the left knee or the right knee that is bothering you?

Pro Tip: Hey Sam, neither of those worked! Try this the next day.

Text 1 "Hey Sam, did you have a chance to check out our Knee program on our website?"

1 min later Text 2 "Here's the link... Do you have time to chat today?"

Meet them- Approach #2 Qualify

The goal of qualifying is to request a prospect to "make the first move".

You Call Me- Text 1 "Thanks for reaching out to us, Sam! It's Jacob. Give me a call at 555-555-5555 and we'll get you right in for your knee appointment! These appointments are limited and highly sought after as Dr. Bradley is an expert in knee pain care. He will listen to you and help you find real relief from your pain. I look forward to talking to you shortly."

Qualify- Text 1 " Hi Sam, it's Jacob from PS Clinic, thanks for reaching out." Text 2 "Our Knee Restore program has about an 85% success rate and has helped a lot of people. To see if you're a good fit I'd like to ask a few questions, is now a bad time?"

Meet them- Approach #3 Commit

The goal here is to get a person scheduled upfront. Once you have done this, positively reinforce this action with a call (preferred) or a text.

Get Scheduled- Text 1 "You did it, Sam! I'm Heather, and it's my job to find a day and time that works best for you. What day of the week usually works best for you? Mornings or afternoons? Text me back or just give me a call at 555-555-5555. Thanks so much!"

The Follow-up Schedule- Text 1 "Hey Sam, I know a lot of people like to schedule them-selves. Here's a link if you'd rather do that: www.youramazinglink.com"

Text 2 "Look forward to seeing you soon!"

LEAD FOLLOW UP PROTOCOL

Objective:
To increase our lead contact rate as well as improve our show-up rate. Lead appointment numbers are more likely to increase when people and automations work together.

The Rule of 3:
When you get a prospect to schedule, never make an appointment past 3 days from the date of contact.

Double Call:
Call screening is very common today so adding a second call if a first is unsuccessful has proven to be effective. This tactic is totally reasonable and most prospects have no problems with it.

Tactical Approach:
Call leads within 5 minutes if possible during clinic hours.
Best times to call are between 8am - 10am / 4pm - 6pm.

Day 1: For best results, leads should be called three times per day the first day the lead comes in. First call at desired time (morning, afternoon, evening), then 2 calls are made after the initial call. NOTE: Spread the 2 follow up calls throughout the day. *DON'T LEAVE A MESSAGE.*

Day 2: Two phone calls are made at appropriate times and a message is left with the second phone call.

Day 3: At the very end of the day one phone call is made.
*NOTE: For ease of use and staff communication see the **Daily Marketer Log Sheet** following this protocol.*

Call Script:
See the **Daily Marketer Script** (which you can locate following this protocol.)

Goal:

After we have completed the objectives in each of these protocols our goal is to have an average appointment set rate at or above 60%.

THE DAILY MARKETER SCRIPT

Note Before Starting:

· Make sure the caller is friendly and relatable.
· ALWAYS USE THE SCRIPT.
· Never schedule past 3 days.
· Do not provide too much information on the call.
· Script Training can be seen on the resources page.

Primary Script:

Hi, is Mary there?

Hi Mary, this is Sam calling from XYZ Clinic here in (Location), and I'm calling just to verify I've got the correct info on your form you submitted...

NOTE: Sound upbeat and cheerful.

Option 1: Transition statement: Have I caught you at a bad time?

NOTE: Our goal is to phrase this transition statement in a way where the response is an easy "no"... NOT "yes".

Option 2: Transition statement: I know you're busy, and so am I. But I've got about 2 mins, is that a problem?

The Setup:

Great, so like I said, I just want to follow up with a couple of questions about your (condition) so if the Doctor has a question I can be as helpful as possible. Sound good?

Frame and filter...

Great! So Mary, because we take helping people with (condition) very seriously. In fact, in most cases we are able to help about 85% of folks who struggle with (condition). But that process begins by making sure our program is a fit for you too.

Discovery and mirror...

It looks like you've been having to deal with some (condition) pain and want to see how our program might help.

Can I ask how long you've been struggling with (symptom)?

...Is it better or worse when you (X)?

...What have you tried already?

NOTE: Having your own list of pertinent questions will make this script more powerful. Take a minute and list any additional questions you would like to add here:

- _____
- _____
- _____
- _____

Maximize Responses:

NOTE: Using Maximizing Statements helps establish both the need for help and your ability to provide the best solution. Do not skip this important step.

...That's not good.

...That's not normal.

...Those symptoms are concerning.

Show empathy:

...I know that can be very frustrating.

...It sounds like you could really use a break.

...I'm sorry to hear that.

Certainty and Commit:

So, Mary, as I told you, we take helping people with (condition) seriously, and based on what you've told me, ***I think our clinic will be a perfect fit...***

NOTE: The tone of voice and certainty you deliver here must be authentic.

The next step would be to get you on our schedule so we can get you the help you need.

I've got 9:00 tomorrow morning or 1:30 tomorrow afternoon. And one slot at 8am (the next day).

Which fits best for you?

Closing Boost: "Ok (name) one more thing. If for some reason you're unable to make your appointment, please let us know. We have limited appointment space available for new patients."

Close: Perfect, we look forward to helping you with your (primary complaint) and I'll let the Doctor know we talked and get him informed about your concerns today. Thanks for the nice chat and we'll see you soon.

Best Practices:

Train and Practice every two weeks or as STATS fall: Your script will change the farther you go without training. Your staff will ad lib and make things up based on what they think is appropriate. Consistent training is key.

Less is more: The goal is NOT for the staff to do a mini consultation. It's NOT to give free advice over the phone. NOT a shoulder to cry on. The goal IS to make the appointment.

The Person Who Asks the Questions is in Control: Never answer a question without following up with your own question. It is OK for prospects to ask a question. It's not ok to let them control the conversation.

Common Objections:

Do you accept insurance?

If yes- , "Yes we do, just be sure to bring your insurance card with you on your first visit so we can verify your benefits. When can you come in?"

If no - "Just bring your insurance card with you on your first visit, so we can verify your benefits. What time works better for you?"

Another option - "Great question, the first thing we need to do is to have the doctor evaluate you, from there we will discuss insurance coverage and any out-of-pocket costs. What time works better for you?"

NOTE: Having your own list of objections and responses will make this script more powerful. Take a minute and list any additional responses you would like to add here:

- _____
- _____
- _____
- _____

For 80% of all other questions

"That's a great question. The first step would be to set up a time to come in for a consultation with one of our providers. The consultation is free and we can figure out the best way to help you with your_____. What time works best for you, mornings or afternoons?"

If all else fails, play dumb

"I just do the scheduling, but I'm sure our providers can help you. Let's setup a time so you can meet with them. What time works best for you?"

Implementing the Rule of 3:

You need to get your new patients within 2-3 days or they are not coming in.

"We are booked up through the next month, but we did have a couple of cancellations in the next couple of days and I'd be happy to get you in. Do mornings or afternoons work better for you?

Remember:

Patients want to know two basic things. 1) Can it help me and 2) How much will it cost? When answering questions on the phone you need to know which questions should be answered and which are better deferred to the appointment.

If you answer all of their questions, they are less likely to show.

Note: If you feel you need further training on this topic, watch the "Double Your Show Rate" tutorial on the resource page.

DAILY MARKETER CERTIFICATION

To certify your use and understanding of the Daily Marketer Script, please take time to complete the following tasks.

(Initial upon completion)

1) Watch the Daily Marketer Video Training. _____
   2) Successfully complete a role-play session. _____
   3) Keep a copy at your desk and use it daily. _____

DAILY MARKETER LOG

Instructions: List the days leads on the list below and complete the form as you make contact with the leads. While Patient Streams tracking software has the same information, this document serves as a quick hand-off system between parties as they follow up with prospects.

Note: The log should be filled out daily and updated to accommodate leads who may not have been contacted on the previous day. Eventually those names will fall off this log as you follow the Lead Calling Protocol.

LEADS	DATE	CALL -TIME	APPT- Y/N

SHOW RATE STAT

70% Target

How to increase your new patient show rate with automation & scripting

Mindset: The Show Rate Protocol is designed to help you fill your Practice with new patients as well as strike a good balance with existing patient visits. Our aim should be to maximize earning every hour your practice is open.

Many times, this protocol can see incredible results with small efforts. Relying solely on automation, while powerful, should NOT be your only strategy.

Use the checklist below to ensure quality control as you implement this protocol.

Checklist:

· Appointment Confirmation Protocol (Automation)_____
· Confirmation Call Protocol/Script_____

APPOINTMENT CONFIRMATION PROTOCOL

Objective:

To maintain at least a 70% show rate of scheduled appointments for Day 1 using Patient Stream appointment reminder automation.

Best Practices:

We understand that many clinics employ an Electronic Health Record (EHR) that handles appointment reminders. We recommend that new leads stay inside the Patient Stream software until they become paying patients. Do not forget to implement the Rule of 3 here as well.

Tactical Approach:

Day 1: Immediate notification

Hi, {{contact.first_name}}.

Your (condition) appointment is scheduled for {{appointment.start_time}}.

Please arrive 20 minutes early to complete new patient paperwork.

Our office address is:

{{ location.address }}

Looking forward to meeting you.

1 Day Before:

Hi, {{contact.first_name}}. We're looking forward to meeting you soon and sharing how we help people end (condition) pain for the long haul.

Also, we want to make sure you get here...

Here's our address: {{ location.address }}

Click here to get turn by turn directions via Google Maps: **(Your Link here.)**

Second text Immediately after:

If you need to reschedule please let us know. See you soon.

1Hr. Before Appointment:

Hey {{contact.first_name}}, see you in an hour.

Goal:

By using these tactics in conjunction with automated reminders we should be able to consistently hit a 70% show rate.

If at any time we are not hitting that number we will need to add in a call prior to the appointment. See the **Call Confirmation Call Protocol.**

CALL CONFIRMATION PROTOCOL

Objective:

To maintain at least a 70% show rate of scheduled appointments for Day 1. By using both the Patient Stream Automation and this Call Confirmation Script we will hit that STAT.

Tactical Approach:

Add in 1 call the Day before the appointment to increase show rate.

Call Confirmation Script:

"Hi Mary, it's Sam from ABC Clinic.

I know you're busy but I wanted to touch base really quickly before your appointment with Dr. Smith tomorrow.

You should have received directions on your phone.

Did you get those, or would you like me to send them again?

Great.

Well, the first person you'll be seeing tomorrow will be me so I'm excited to see if we can help.

And one last thing and I'll let you go.

If for any reason you need to change your appointment, please let me know so we can give your appointment slot to others who may be waiting to get in.

Sound good? Great. See ya tomorrow."

Goal:

By using this script in conjunction with automated reminders we should be able to consistently hit a 70% show rate.

DAY 1 PROTOCOLS

Day 1 - Day 2 Stat

80% Target

How to maximize patient enrollment with quality service, pre-framing, and proven scripting.

Mindset: Advancing a new patient from Day 1 to Day 2 starts immediately when a prospect walks in the door. We will help more people by using deliberate communication tactics and meeting folks where they are, not where we want them to be.

This process can take on many different forms, the following protocols are what have proven to work for us.

Required Learning: Unlike the previous protocols, at this stage of the process it is a good idea to take time to educate yourself on the role of communication and about the new patient process. This protocol is meant to guide you through the process but you will need to review the materials provided in New Patient School to receive the full benefit.

If you have difficulty converting Prospects into Patients please go to the **New Patient School** training attached as well as review the video training.

Use the checklist below to ensure quality control as you implement.

Checklist:

· Day 1 Protocol_____
· New Patient School Day 1 Remastered_____

Day 1 Protocol

Objective:

The goal is to increase communication using pre-frame techniques and empathy. From the moment the patient walks through the door until he/she is checked out for their second appointment, the goal is to provide the patient with a VIP experience. We want to be sure to answer any questions or concerns they may have and provide clear answers.

Required Learning:

Before implementing this protocol, or your variation, be sure to review both the video and notes that follow this protocol.

Best Practices:

Adapting this process to fit your needs is a recommended step. It is also recommended that scripts be written to go along with the process. When staff vary too far away from scripting, our results will also fall.

OFFICE SCRIPTING

OFFICE FLOW **USER KEY:**

FD - Front Desk; CM - Case Manager; C - Chiropractor NP or C- Nurse Practitioner/MD or Chiro

STEP-BY-STEP DAY 1:

___ **(FD)**   Welcome the new patient into the office and point out where the restrooms and water fountains are.

___ **(FD)**   Get a clipboard. Place the **Welcome Packet** form on the clipboard. Give it to the new patient with a pen.

___ **(FD)**   Ask the patient for an insurance card and some type of photo ID (driver license preferred). ***This step is vital.***

___ **(FD)**   Make a copy back and front of the insurance card and ID then return to patient.

___ **(FD)**   Ask the patient to have a seat and fill out the welcome packet.

___ **(FD)**   After the patient returns the clipboard to the front desk, you will need to collect payment (primary care copay for medical). Ask them to have a seat and we will be with them shortly.

___ **(FD)**   Fill out the name of the patient, date, and Office Ally patient # on every page of the Initial Intake Exam packet and Welcome Packet.

___ **(FD)**   Make a copy of Welcome Packet front page and place it in the insurance verification box for the days verification of benefits.

___ **(FD)**   Place a Consultation sheet on the clipboard and place the clipboard in the Case Manager's box.

___ **(FD)** The Case Manager (or Front Desk) will then take the patient to the consultation room while giving them a tour of the office on the way back to the consultation room.

___ **(CM)** Case Manager grabs clinic director/chiropractor for introduction.

___ **(C)** Chiropractor/director introduces himself/herself to the patient, **confirms goals and PMH (past medical history), re-affirms they are in the right place and that we are going to get them in front of our medical provider for a work up.**

___ **(CM)** The Case Manager completes the **subjective portion** of the Consultation, handles any questions or objections to receiving care (about 7 minutes long).

___ **(CM)** While the consultation takes place, it is best practice to verify the benefits of the insurance (otherwise, insurance should be called at the end of shift).

___ **(CM)** If your clinic is offering an initial treatment, make sure the patient receives a session before they leave the office.

___ **(CM)** After the consultation is over the CM will leave the consultation room to make sure the medical provider is ready to see the patient. The new patient chart will be handed over for the medical provider to review. During this time the CM will relay pertinent information that the medical provider should be aware of.

___ **(NP) (C)** The provider will review the patient's chart before seeing the patient.

___ **(CM)** The CM walks the patient to the provider/exam room and introduces them to the provider.

___ **(NP) (C)** The provider will perform **a problem focused exam** and take any necessary x-rays.

___ **(NP) (C)** The provider will close out the exam and prepare the patient for their Day 2 visit.

___ **(CM)** (a) The case manager will come in for closing remarks and schedule the patient for their day 2 visit while in the exam room.

___ **(NP) (C)** (b) The provider will walk the patient to the front desk to schedule their Day 2 visit and hand the patient off to the front desk for scheduling of day 2.

___ **(NP) (C)** The provider will call the patient at the end of the day to confirm we can help and to follow-up with the knee decompression session - if performed.

___ **(CM)** After having received the provider's recommendations for care, the case manager preps the care plan and verifies insurance benefits.

Overview: This document serves as notes to the video training you will find at the link below. These are here so you can follow along and make notes as you learn.

Video Training: https://www.mypatientstream.com/school/

DAY 1 REMASTERED

What We Will Cover:

1 - Patient Experience
2 - Pre-framing to increase enrollments
3 - Three things you MUST know

1 - Patient Experience Today

QUESTION - If I walked into your practice today, what is the very first thing that 80% of clinics do wrong when handling patients?

Notes:

Making a good first impression - When thinking about customer service and making a good first impression, understand it is a big deal. People will make judgements within the first 3 minutes. Think more like the Ritz Carlton and NOT Red Roof Inn.

· Anticipate their arrival - We have a 5 minute "huddle" to get ready for the patients walking in for the day. When a new face walks in and it is their scheduled time say, "Hi! You must be Jane. I'm Heather and it's so great to have you in our office!" Welcome that person as if this is a close friend's grandmother. Make it genuine. Make sure you're authentic and make them feel welcome. Let them know what the next step will be. EX: Welcome to the office. Here's our new patient paperwork, fill it out, it will take about 10 mins. If you have your ID or insurance please get it ready so we can check out your benefits. If you need to use the restroom the bathroom is over here.

We have some water bottles if you're thirsty, etc.

· Make them feel welcome - Look at your patients like "this is someone's mother, or someone's child and how would they want me to treat them?". We train our staff on how to handle these people and we practice/role play scenarios. Do not just let your front desk staff "wing it". Train and role play on customer service. The companies that do customer service really well train and practice it.

Notes:

· Show don't tell – Do not just say "the elevator is the second door on the right". Walk them there. If a patient needs to use the restroom, walk them to the restroom.

· Office Tour - What are you known for? You can make a big impact on patients who are just coming into the office for the first time. They will see people getting adjustments as we walk back to the exam room. While this happens, we inform them what is going on. We inform them about how the doctor is unique and what makes him/her a great choice for ailments. What makes your office special? 30 second commercial from your staff as they escort your patients to their room. Think - dinner guest. You would take a house tour to make them feel more comfortable. Same with an office tour. Another thing a successful doctor does is have a success wall full of people the doctor has helped. Severe cases that have been helped is great for this as well. "If they can help that person they can help me". Showcase awesome case studies.

· Go the extra "inch" - All these little things are free to do. These are tiny things that make your patient feel great. EX: After a patient exam, the Doctor calls his patients and says, "Thanks for coming in today. I had a chance to look over your exam and X-rays and worked up a treatment plan that I think is really going to work for you. Thank you for coming in and we'll talk more about it at your next appointment."

Notes:

· STORY: I've been to the Ritz Carlton twice. I did not do that just to spend a lot of money on a hotel, but I wanted my staff and my team to understand what good customer service looks like. I told my staff 1) Take a mental note on how you feel when you walk in. 2) Take notes on what things they are doing to make you feel welcome. 3) Ask them to do something for you and see what they do. My staff was amazed at their staff's level of service. When they saw my kids, the staff said "Hey do you want to check out our candy table?". The staff asked us politely if they could give our kids some candy. Tactically, what they were doing was freeing me up to check in at the front desk lobby while distracting my kids. They were very kind about it. We were helped right away. They knew we were there before and had some of our preferences in their system. They knew the temperature of our room. They knew we didn't like our sheets tucked at the bottom. After being in the room for 5 minutes, they knocked on the door and were checking to see if there was anything that we wanted. He looked at my son and asked him, "Sir, is there anything I can get you?" My son said "I'd love some bubble water. And some cheese crackers." He responded with, "I'm not sure if we have cheese crackers but I'm sure we can figure something out for you". He came back with goldfish crackers. All done with kindness. These are some strategies and patterns that you can implement in the office. Guaranteed the Ritz Carlton trains on this.

· Just like the Ritz, we are always anticipating their arrival.

Notes:

2 - Pre-framing to increase enrollments

· Always explain one step ahead in the process - This is true for both doctor and front desk staff.
· STORY: I once went to a chiropractor who said "Lay down" and started adjusting me. It was jarring and I felt like I didn't know what was going on.
· What to do instead – "I'm going to do some adjustments, it's going to feel like this, I'll let you know when I'm going to do it so you'll be ready."

· MANAGE EXPECTATIONS: EX: Picture of a woman in knee decompression machine - How would you pre-frame this? Role play this! Not every patient is going to be instantly better. You need to prepare them for what the possible outcomes could be. Manage this expectation. EX: "What we are going to do here is to gently move your knee, which will allow fluid to move into your joint. Then, one of three things may happen – 1) you may feel a bit sore because you've been dealing with this for 3 years 2) you may feel nothing. This is completely normal as it can take more than 1 treatment to fix your issue 3) You may feel like I just waived a magic wand and that you want to run around the block. Please don't do that! As we still need to do some treatments to continue the therapy."

Notes:

· You can pre-frame your phone calls, your visits, etc. Implement this more in your office. Confusion is the enemy to conversion. Pre-Framing is a great way to expel confusion. Help them understand what to expect.

· Examples:
   ◦ After you finish your paperwork, we'll take you to the consultation room.
   ◦ After your consultation, we'll have you meet with our doctor.
   ◦ After your exam, we'll setup a time to review your results with you.

○ On your next visit we will review your x-rays, go over recommendations, your insurance coverage, any out-of-pocket costs, etc.

PATIENTS WANT TO KNOW WHAT YOU ARE THINKING - TELL THEM! When you're transparent and honest with your patients, they will appreciate that.

· NOTE - Pre-framing typically takes place during transitions.

· Do not give all this information away at once. Parcel it out. Ex: Someone calls up and asks, "how are you guys going to help me?" Respond with, "Well let me tell you, our doctor is amazing, we're going to take you in and we'll get your paperwork done, you'll meet with the doctor, then we'll have you come back later with your spouse, etc." Do not divulge the entire process! Take it step by step and piece by piece.

· ***This is stuff you MUST train weekly on. If it seems too overwhelming to you, take one transition at a time. Work on it then move to the next.

Notes:

3 - Three things you MUST know - The top 3 things clinics must do to get new patients

1. Niche offers - One of the ways that businesses get new patients is new offers. Put things in front of people that makes them stop, grabs their attention, and gets them to read. The enemy to niche offers is thinking that a "commodity offer" is a niche offer. Marketing to People that have a specific issue, not just a general chiropractic issue, will serve you well.

2. Regularly scheduled training - Is your staff winging it? Are they scripted? Are you having to micromanage? You do not need to be a micromanager but you should train your staff twice a week. Pre-frame this for your staff. "On Tuesday, we will be training on phone scripts. So, everyone have your scripts down and we'll practice." It will make your staff feel like they are doing their job the right way because you have told

them how to do it. Make it fun! Pay them for their training. Bring in lunch from time to time. Make games out of it, give out Starbucks gift cards. Make it fun.

3. How to massively increase new patient enrollments and conversions - DON'T GIVE AWAY TOO MUCH INFORMATION- Especially after an exam or over the phone. Your stats will start to sink. Let the enrollment process (Day 1, Day 2) do the work. If you are giving away all your information at once your patient will make a decision whether or not they want to follow through with care based on the knowledge and feeling that they currently have. If you give too much info it may seem like a lot of work, or that it is going to take too much time. If you tell the patient, "We can help you in 36 months" but they have another doctor that says they can help in 1 treatment they will take the 1 day. They do not have a frame of reference on why your care will take that long. Do not give them too much information, even if they are asking for it. EX: "I have back problems; how long will it take to fix?" Your response, "That's a great question. The first step will be to have you come into our office. We'll have our doctor take a look at you and he/she can help answer that for you. When can you come in, mornings or afternoons?".

Notes:

NEW PATIENT ENROLLMENT STAT

80% Target

How to maximize new patient conversions with clear communication, proper positioning, and problem-solving choices

Mindset: Most people overthink the enrollment process. As long as we have done a good job on Day 1, Day 2 is much simpler.

This is because when it comes to making big decisions, the human brain follows a predictable formula. Our brains make 80% of our decisions based on emotions first and the remaining 20% based on logic.

So, if you have a difficult time enrolling new patients think about the "subjective experience" new patients have on Day 1. If you still have a problem, focus on communication during Day 2. Make sure you provide clear solutions and viable options for people to take action.

Required Learning: Much like Day 1, it is a good idea to take time to educate yourself on the role of communication, proper positioning, and scripting as it pertains to Day 2. Review the materials provided in New Patient School to receive the full benefit of this protocol.

See the attached notes and video resources to learn more.

Use the checklist below to ensure quality control as you implement.

Checklist:

- Day 2 Protocol_____
- How to Enroll Patients Without "High-Pressure" Sales Tactics_____

DAY 2 PROTOCOL

Objective:

Before presenting a care plan for future visits, you need to ensure that the patient is committed and on board with the treatment plan. The patient should have absolutely no more questions left. If there is even an ounce of confusion, the patient will not start care.

Situations that create confusion:

The areas *below* need to be addressed before a care plan is presented. If the patient is not fully in agreement in all 6 categories, do not proceed to the care plan.

- Benefits and insurance coverage
- Length of care
- Cost of care
- Short-term versus long-term care
- Relief care versus corrective care
- Future benefits of care

OFFICE SCRIPTING

OFFICE FLOW **USER KEY:**

FD - Front Desk; CM - Case Manager; C - Chiropractor NP or C- Nurse Practitioner/MD or Chiro

DAY 2:

___ **(FD)** Front desk greets the patient and spouse by name.

___ **(FD)** Confirm the consultation room is ready with x-rays ready to view.

___ **(FD)** Front desk/CM walks the patient to the consultation room and starts the ROF.

___ **(NP) (C)** Provider will review the patient's primary complaint, x-ray, and exam findings and answer any clinical questions related to the x-rays or problem (5 minutes or less). Build excitement!

Possible Scripting:
   "(Name) I'm glad you came to our office and chose the wellness approach. Most conventional approaches like urgent care, hospitals, and pain clinics just look to mask your symptoms with medication or surgery. Before 2-3 weeks are over patients have spent **$6-8k** on their care with no real results. Our goal is to go directly to the underlying cause."

   (WE INTENTIONALLY PUT A DOLLAR VALUE IN THEIR HEAD.)

Positioning Script:
   Provider: "Jim, what do you think will happen with your (Problem) if you do absolutely nothing?"
   Patient: "It will get worse."
   Provider: "That's true. If problems like this are left untreated they will get worse."
   (If the answer is, "it will get worse," proceed to second question.)
   Gauge Commitment:

"Jim, on a scale of 1 to 10, where is your commitment. 10 being you are willing to do whatever it takes and one being you are able to live with this pain and do not want to do much in terms of correcting it."

Answer: 10/10

(Make sure their commitment is a 9 or 10 before you proceed to Financial.)

Certainty and Commit:

"Good, I'm glad you are a 10 out of 10 for commitment because there is help and there is hope. We can help. If we are more excited about your care than you are, Jim, this never works. There has to be a bigger commitment on your part. You need to make your visits and commit to your home care exercises. There also is a commitment in terms of finances and I'll have (name) go over that with you now."

___ **(NP) (C)** The Provider will hand off to the CM to complete the ROF including reviewing exam findings, treatment recommendations, insurance coverage, and out of pocket charges.

NOTE: If the patient is reluctant, they will put up barriers and find reasons not to start care. *Look at their mannerisms and body language.*

Increase Your Communication:

- Describe in detail what is included in their care plan and relate the feature back to their problem (This will plant visual ideas and increase value of care).

- Communicate the benefit first then follow it with the feature.

Example: In your Neuropathy treatment plan we will include:

"Ok John, our main goal here is to decrease your pain, and restore function. In order to do that we need to start by waking-up your nerve cells. We are going to do this with 15 Class IV laser sessions, and you'll get one at each of your visits. Have you used a Class IV laser before? "

(Use follow-up questions to bring people along and gauge interest.)

"Next we want to restore circulation. So, to increase circulation and start sending more nutrients to your nerves we're going to include 20 Acupuncture sessions as well. This approach is great because we will immediately start the repair process. Are you starting to see how this approach is more beneficial than just medicating to mask symptoms?"

(IT'S RECOMMENDED TO WALK THEM THROUGH THE OFFICE AND SHOW THEM WHERE EACH OF THESE SERVICE CENTERS ARE, THIS BUILDS VALUE IN EACH SPECIFIC SERVICE CENTER.)

Transition Statements:

"Do you understand why we do laser, acupuncture, (other services included with plan)?"
(Make sure they completely understand every modality before you proceed to financial.)

"Money aside, is this something you would want to do"

Patient: "Yes"

"Great, we never let finances stop patients from starting care; we even have an affordable financing program."

___ **(CM)** The CM will present a treatment schedule and payment plan with the patient (cash, credit card, financing).

___ **(CM)** The CM will walk the patient to the front desk to complete the Day 2 checkout procedure.

___ **(NP) (C)** Patient will receive initial treatment.

___ **(FD)** The patient is reminded of their next appointment with enthusiasm and a high level of energy and thanked for coming in for this visit before leaving the office.

___ **(NP) (C)** After the end of the day the medical provider will call the patient to check in on how they are feeling after their first treatment.

New Patient School Lecture

Overview: This documents serves as notes to the video training you will find at the link below. These are here so you can follow along and make notes as you learn.

Video Training: https://www.mypatientstream.com/school/

DAY 2: ENROLL NEW PATIENTS WITHOUT "HIGH-PRESSURE" TACTICS.

Overview:

1. Review findings
2. Confirm the patient understands the problem
3. Review options
4. Review your recommendations
5. Provide financial options

3 Concepts you will walk away with today:

1. Be positioned as an expert giving advice and not a sales pitch
2. Learn the phrases, transition statements, and triggers proven to enroll patients ethically
3. Help your team onboard more new patients by following a proven system.

Where should the patient be at this point:

· They have been through a systemized Day 1 with consult/exam.
· They should have some hope and sense that you can help.

They have had some patient education between Day 1 and the ROF (a day 2 video).

FIVE STEP REPORT OF FINDINGS

5 Step ROF Formula

1. Pre-frame what is about to happen
2. Review results from Day 1
3. Confirm they understand and want help
4. Make recommendations
5. Review financial

1 – Pre-Frame

PRE-FRAMING STORY - A month ago, I went into my dentist for a cleaning. They took a few X-rays as one of my molars was chipped. "Yep, you need a root canal, we need to remove it". I'm not a big fan of root canals so I said I didn't really need that tooth so just remove it. I went in a week later. They took my blood pressure and it was very high, like emergency level high. "Why is it that high?" "You're nervous. Let me tell you what's going on today and maybe that will help you calm down." She went ahead and told me what was going to happen today and that they do this all of the time. Taking the tooth out is not difficult and you'll be just fine. She then took my blood pressure again and it was significantly lower!

Imagine that your patient is coming back for Day 2. They may have a look of concern. Maybe they are concerned about finances, if this treatment can help, etc. BEFORE you talk about their treatment or payment, start off with telling them about what you are going to discuss. Help to calm them and make them feel at ease. Small talk with them and get to know them a bit.

"Ok (name), here's the plan for today: The first thing we're going to do is go through what we found on your first visit (x rays, lab testing, etc). Then I'll show you what we found and help you understand what's causing your specific issue. After that we'll discuss what therapy we can provide to help you, and then we'll talk about finances and how much it's going to cost."

When you pre-frame like this, you are essentially "removing the sale". By pre-framing, you are helping that person get on your same page and take them out of where they are in their mind. It is essentially getting their permission to continue.

It is simple and takes a minute or so to do, BUT just because it is simple, it does not make it any less important. Please do not skip over this step!

A great ender, "We see this problem all of the time. We get great results. I'm going to show you how we get those results in a minute."

Notes:

2 - Review Results from Day 1

Give examples of what looks good and what looks bad. You should have done some of this in an education process (EX- what knee degeneration looks like). They should have a sense already. Then, on Day 2, I pull up their X-ray and a degeneration chart. I then ask them what they see and then I am quiet. You want to make sure your patient education process is working. If they give you a correct answer, *"Yes, that's right."* If they give you a wrong answer, *"I see how you could think that but you're actually here..."*

We want them to verbalize their issue.

Talk about their past treatments. Do not make them feel stupid or bad about any past treatments that they have received. Help them understand that you are going to do something different.

IE: *"The reason cortisone shots haven't fixed the problem is because it just temporarily reduces inflammation. Once the shot wears off, you're right back to where you started or worse."*

Notes:

3 - Confirm they understand the problem

1 - Do you see why you are having knee pain?
2 - What do you think will happen if you do not address this problem?
3 - Do you want to fix it?

****DON'T ANSWER THE QUESTION FOR THEM! Let them answer****
Be ok with a bit of silence while they are thinking. When you ask them it engages their mind.

If your patient gets side tracked and does not answer the question and goes in another direction go with them. Always bring them back to answer the question. You can not move forward until they have answered them.

EX: If the patient answers the question with another question, answer their question and then go back to your original question.

Notes:

4 - Make Recommendations:
Special Note

If the patient came in for a special promotion (EX: covered by Medicare) make sure you avoid the "bait and switch" objection. "You said this was covered by Medicare!" You can do this by pre-framing. "Hey, we have some great options that are covered by Medicare, but we also have some therapies that would be great for you that aren't covered by Medicare. Would it be ok with you to walk you through these so you know ALL of your options?" ASK for permission.

Notes:

How we make our recommendations

We go through the therapy, having good communication by explaining this:
    1 - Feature
    2 - Advantage
    3 - Benefit

EX: "This is therapy number 1. This is how it works. The advantage of this care is _____. The benefit for you with this care is_____."
This helps to apply it to their specific issue. Make sure you do not skip the benefit part!

EX – "We are going to inject you with Hyaluronic acid. It is an injection that puts... What this does for you will relieve your pain and help you to walk longer without as much pain... This therapy is covered by your insurance and I'll show you in a minute what your costs are for that. The other therapy is a knee brace. This provides support and care for your knee while you're getting injections. It will relieve wear and tear on your knee and will help alleviate pressure. We also have the knee decompression machine. This is the machine we had you do on day 1. The goal of knee decompression is to open up your bones and allow space for the other therapies to work more effectively. It also takes stress off your knee to reduce pain. Regenerative therapy is another part of the therapy we can include. What it does is...How it would benefit you is..."

A good tactic is to include other well thought of surgeries that are not covered by insurance, like Lasik eye surgery. This is not covered by insurance, but it should be, just like this regenerative medicine.

Notes:

Review Financials

When going over financial recommendations go through the plan line by line while covering up the next line ahead. If you are using a care plan that they are looking at, cover each line and section and only leave open the sections that you are going over with them.

EX: Knee Visco-supplementation - Copay - Coinsurance - # of Visits - Total

"This is the total. How would you like to pay for that? Cash, Credit Card or Check?"

AND THEN BE QUIET!

Another Option "WE have a few options. You can pay in total with cash, credit card or check. You can pay half down and half later. We can do a monthly option. We also have patient financing (care credit) which will come out to about $150 a month. Which one of these makes most sense for you?"

AND THEN BE QUIET!

***If you have done your Day 1 and Day 2 processes correctly, this ending should not be too difficult or stressful of a process. 80% of the people that stick around should be willing to work out a payment at this point.

If someone is really struggling with the price say, "Listen, we never want price to be a reason somebody does not get the help they need. So, we can talk about some other options, fair enough?"

Notes:

IF they really cannot afford it, consider modifying the offer:

· Remove a service?
· Just do insurance-based therapies?
· Less visits?

Get creative and have an honest dialogue with your patients on helping them understand what they can do versus just accepting that they "can't afford it" and letting them walk out the door.

There are 2 Camps of thought/Care for where patients are at with their care and what they are looking for.

1 - I really need some relief. The pain is bothering me. All I care about is relief.
2 - Resolution - Fixing the problem permanently

EX: "These are your options. This is what your insurance covers. This is an option that insurance partially covers and some out of pocket. This is how to fix this short term and this is how to fix this permanently."

Notes:

DOCTOR VS. CASE MANAGER

Who should be doing the ROF?

"For years and years I was the one doing it. I didn't love doing it, but I knew I could close at 80%. Then we started training a case manager. Our office got too busy and I couldn't do all of the ROF's. She was trained, scripted, and shadowed me for a few months. Then we let her do it and she actually closed more than me. It was rare that someone would walk out without signing up. "

"The reason I like case managers doing this is because they have less skin in the game. Chiropractors have bills, costs, etc. But case managers don't have that emotional component connected to it, creating a calmer scenario."

"This is Tammy, She's our case manager. I've reviewed all of your needs with her. She knows what she's doing. She's an expert and can answer any questions you have".

"I would transfer the idea of an "expert" mindset of my patients to her. She has borrowed credibility from the doctor." - Dr. Andrew Wells

If you are hiring a case manager, make sure that you have the right personality for that role-happy, kind, outgoing, warm. Do not hire an analytical type to do your ROF's.

Here is a great resource for your interviewees. Have them take a personality test to find out how they operate: https://www.16personalities.com/

Notes:

www.ingramcontent.com/pod-product-compliance
Lightning Source LLC
Chambersburg PA
CBHW081747200326
41597CB00024B/4416